A Burns Experience

Songs and poems of Robert Burns

Edited by Elizabeth Hepburn

ISBN-10: 0957341520

ISBN-13: 978-0-9573415-2-4

CONTENTS

Poems

INTRODUCTION

Robert Burns (25 January 1759 – 21 July 1796) is also known as Rabbie Burns, Scotland's favourite son, the Ploughman Poet, the Bard of Ayrshire and in Scotland as simply *The Bard.* He is widely regarded as the greatest of Scotland's poets and lyricists, and is celebrated throughout the world and across many cultures.

He is considered to be a pioneer of the Romantic movement, striking out from the popular ideals of 'The Enlightenment' towards a more personal and artistic verse. His writings of Ae Fond Kiss and My Love is like a Red Red Rose are typical examples of this. As an icon of Scotland, Burns soon became something of a cultural phenomenon, inspiring literature events to this day across the globe. The song, Scots Wha Hae was the unofficial national anthem of Scotland for many years.

Of all his work, Auld Lang Syne is probably the most recognized; Burns wrote the poem to a song taken from an old Scots dance. It is most commonly heard on New Year's Day in the Western world. Variations of it can be heard by school children in China to signify friendship, and in Japan when restaurants wish their patrons to exit at the end of the day. Other poems and songs of Burns that remain well-known today include A Man's A Man for A' That, To a Louse, and To a Mouse.

Burns also collected folk songs from across Scotland, often revising or adapting them. His works are iconic to Scottish literature, and are still held in the highest regard.

Songs

1

AE FOND KISS

Considered by many to be the ultimate love song, *Ae Fond Kiss* is a dedication to Burns' love of the separated Clarinda (Nancy) Macklehose. The two exchanged many letters of affection but were not able to engage in an open love affair. When Macklehose left Scotland, Burns wrote this as a farewell to her.

Ae fond kiss, and then we sever;
Ae fareweel, alas, for ever!
Deep in heart-wrung tears I'll pledge thee,
Warring sighs and groans I'll wage thee.
Who shall say that Fortune grieves him,
While the star of hope she leaves him?
Me, nae cheerful twinkle lights me;
Dark despair around benights me.

I'll ne'er blame my partial fancy,
Naething could resist my Nancy:
But to see her was to love her;
Love but her, and love for ever.
Had we never lov'd sae kindly,
Had we never lov'd sae blindly,
Never met-or never parted,
We had ne'er been broken-hearted.

Fare-thee-weel, thou first and fairest!
Fare-thee-weel, thou best and dearest!
Thine be ilka joy and treasure,
Peace, Enjoyment, Love and Pleasure!
Ae fond kiss, and then we sever!
Ae fareweel alas, for ever!
Deep in heart-wrung tears I'll pledge thee,
Warring sighs and groans I'll wage thee.

2

A MAN'S A MAN FOR A' THAT

First published in 1795, *A Man's A Man For A' That* was sent in anonymously to The Glasgow Magazine and is Burn's most famous political song. To this day it strikes such a chord that it was sung at the opening of The Scottish Parliament in 1999.

Is there for honest poverty
That hangs his head, an' a' that
The coward slave, we pass him by
We dare be poor for a' that
For a' that, an' a' that
Our toil's obscure and a' that
The rank is but the guinea's stamp
The man's the gowd for a' that

What though on hamely fare we dine
Wear hoddin grey, an' a' that
Gie fools their silks, and knaves their wine
A man's a man, for a' that
For a' that, an' a' that
Their tinsel show an' a' that
The honest man, though e'er sae poor
Is king o' men for a' that

Ye see yon birkie ca'd a lord
Wha struts an' stares an' a' that
Tho' hundreds worship at his word
He's but a coof for a' that
For a' that, an' a' that
His ribband, star and a' that
The man o' independent mind
He looks an' laughs at a' that

A prince can mak' a belted knight
A marquise, duke, an' a' that
But an honest man's aboon his might
Gude faith, he maunna fa' that
For a' that an' a' that
Their dignities an' a' that

The pith o' sense an' pride o' worth
Are higher rank that a' that

Then let us pray that come it may
(as come it will for a' that)
That Sense and Worth, o'er a' the earth
Shall bear the gree an' a' that
For a' that an' a' that
It's coming yet for a' that
That man to man, the world o'er
Shall brithers be for a' that.

3

MY LUVE IS LIKE A RED RED ROSE

Written around 1794, the song was for Burns' then wife, Jean Armour. The Song conveys a sense that love can transcend the furthest borders and time. It is frequently played for Valentine's Day and weddings.

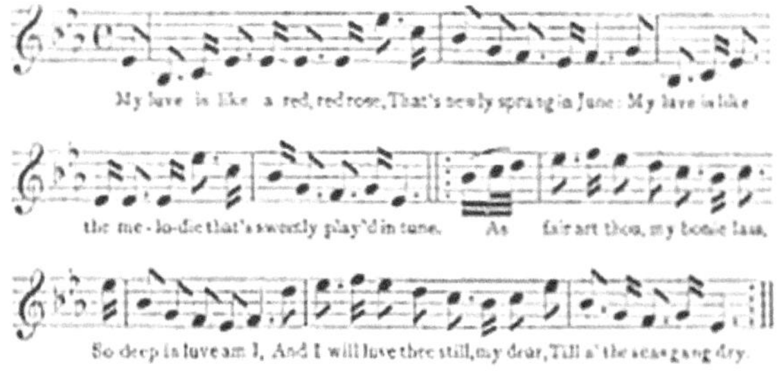

O my Luve's like a red, red rose,
That's newly sprung in June:
O my Luve's like the melodie,
That's sweetly play'd in tune.

As fair art thou, my bonie lass,
So deep in luve am I;
And I will luve thee still, my dear,
Till a' the seas gang dry.

Till a' the seas gang dry, my dear,
And the rocks melt wi' the sun;
And I will luve thee still, my dear,
While the sands o' life shall run.

And fare-thee-weel, my only Luve!
And fare-thee-weel, a while!
And I will come again, my Luve,
Tho' 'twere ten thousand mile!

4

SCOTS WHA HAE

Scots Wha Hae was written after Burns visited the site of Bannockburn, the historic battlefield where Robert The Bruce fought back and won against the English in 1314. He submitted it anonymously in 1793 in an attempt to protect himself from retribution from the authorities of the time.

Scots, wha hae wi' Wallace bled,
Scots, wham Bruce has aften led,
Welcome to your gory bed,
Or to Victorie!

Now's the day, and now's the hour;
See the front o' battle lour;
See approach proud Edward's power-
Chains and Slaverie!

Wha will be a traitor knave?
Wha can fill a coward's grave?
Wha sae base as be a Slave?
Let him turn and flee!

Wha, for Scotland's King and Law,
Freedom's sword will strongly draw,
Free-man stand, or Free-man fa',
Let him on wi' me!

By Oppression's woes and pains!
By your Sons in servile chains!
We will drain our dearest veins,
But they shall be free!

Lay the proud Usurpers low!
Tyrants fall in every foe!
Liberty's in every blow!
Let us Do or Die!

5

COMIN' THRO THE RYE

One of the Bard's more raunchy offerings, *Comin' Thro' The Rye* reflects the outlook of the times when romance in the young was frowned upon. This is one of the most characteristic of all Burns Songs, although one of his earliest written in 1784.

Gin a body meet a body
Comin' thro' the rye
Gin a body kiss a body
Need a body cry?
Ilka lassie has her laddie
Nane, they say, ha'e I
Yet a' the lads they smile at me
When comin' thro' the Rye.

Gin a body meet a body
Comin' frae the town
Gin a body greet a body
Need a body frown
Ilka lassie has her laddie
Nane, they say, ha'e I
Yet a' the lads they lo'e me weel
When comin' thro' the Rye.

Amang the train, there is a swain
I dearly lo'e mysel'
But whaur his hame, or what his name
I dinna care to tell
Every lassie has her laddie
Nane, they say, ha'e I
Yet a' the lads they lo'e me weel
When comin' thro' the Rye.

6

MY HEART'S IN THE HIGHLANDS

While written before the infamous Highland clearances of 1814, Burns' song (originally written in 1789) evokes the feelings of those on the verge of the event and has long been played in memory of the act.

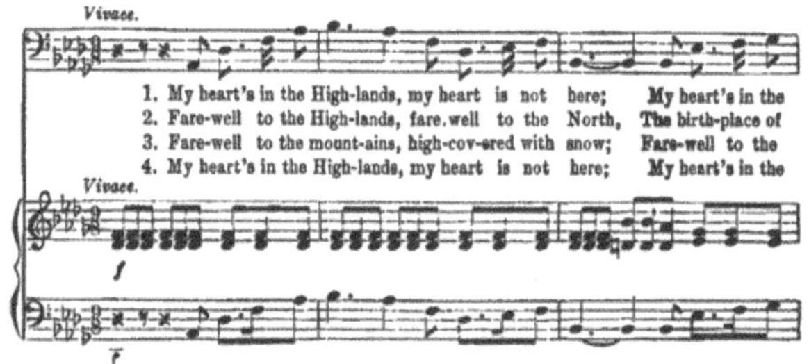

My heart's in the Highlands, my heart is not here,
My heart's in the Highlands, a-chasing the deer;
Chasing the wild-deer, and following the roe,
My heart's in the Highlands, wherever I go.

Farewell to the Highlands, farewell to the North,
The birth-place of Valour, the country of Worth ;
Wherever I wander, wherever I rove,
The hills of the Highlands for ever I love.

Farewell to the mountains, high-cover'd with snow,
Farewell to the straths and green vallies below;
Farewell to the forests and wild-hanging woods,
Farewell to the torrents and loud-pouring floods
.

My heart's in the Highlands, my heart is not here,
My heart's in the Highlands, a-chasing the deer;
Chasing the wild-deer, and following the roe,
My heart's in the Highlands, wherever I go.

7

GREEN GROW THE RASHES

Often recited during Burns Suppers, *Green Grow The Rashes* is thought to have been based on an ancient ballad first set down in 1549. The song is still popular with musicians today.

There's nought but care on ev'ry han',
In every hour that passes, O:
What signifies the life o' man,
An' 'twere na for the lasses, O.

Chorus: Green grow the rashes, O;
Green grow the rashes, O;
The sweetest hours that e'er I spend,
Are spent among the lasses, O.

The war'ly race may riches chase,
An' riches still may fly them, O;
An' tho' at last they catch them fast,
Their hearts can ne'er enjoy them, O.
Chorus: Green grow the rashes, O;
Green grow the rashes, O;
The sweetest hours that e'er I spend,
Are spent among the lasses, O.

But gie me a cannie hour at e'en,
My arms about my dearie, O,
An' war'ly cares an' war'ly men
May a' gae tapsalteerie, O!
Chorus: Green grow the rashes, O;
Green grow the rashes, O;
The sweetest hours that e'er I spend,
Are spent among the lasses, O.

For you sae douce, ye sneer at this;
Ye're nought but senseless asses, O;

The wisest man the warl' e'er saw,
He dearly lov'd the lasses, O.
Chorus: Green grow the rashes, O;
Green grow the rashes, O;
The sweetest hours that e'er I spend,
Are spent among the lasses, O.

Auld Nature swears, the lovely dears
Her noblest work she classes, O:
Her prentice han' she try'd on man,
An' then she made the lasses, O.
Chorus: Green grow the rashes, O;
Green grow the rashes, O;
The sweetest hours that e'er I spend,
Are spent among the lasses, O.

JOHN ANDERSON MY JO

Burns' tribute to lifelong affection is a less bawdy version of an older song describing the effects of aging on the body. In this adaptation the Bard plays with the idea of love across a lifetime.

John Anderson, my jo, John,
When we were first acquent;
Your locks were like the raven,
Your bonie brow was brent;
But now your brow is beld, John,
Your locks are like the snaw;
But blessings on your frosty pow,
John Anderson, my jo!

John Anderson, my jo, John,
We clamb the hill thegither;
And mony a cantie day, John,
We've had wi' ane anither:
Now we maun totter down, John,
And hand in hand we'll go,
And sleep thegither at the foot,
John Anderson, my jo!

9

THE BANKS O' DOON

Better known as *'Ye Banks and Braes O Bonnie Doon'*, this famous love song was written in 1791 for Johnson's Musical Museum. The themes of love and regret follow through as strongly as the imagery of the River Doon in Ayrshire in which it is set.

Ye banks and braes o' bonnie Doon,
How can ye bloom sae fresh and fair?
How can ye chant, ye little birds,
And I sae weary fu' o' care!
Thou'll break my heart, thou warbling bird,
That wantons thro' the flowering thorn:
Thou minds me o' departed joys,
Departed never to return.

Aft hae I rov'd by Bonnie Doon,
To see the rose and woodbine twine:
And ilka bird sang o' its Luve,
And fondly sae did I o' mine;
Wi' lightsome heart I pu'd a rose,
Fu' sweet upon its thorny tree!
And may fause Luver staw my rose,
But ah! he left the thorn wi' me.

10

AFTON WATER

One of Burns' most popular songs, this gently rippling tune, which Burns is believed to have sent to the Scots Musical Museum, matches the lyric exquisitely.

Flow gently sweet Afton, among thy green braes,
Flow gently, I'll sing thee a song in thy praise;
My Mary's asleep by thy murmuring stream,
Flow gently, sweet Afton, disturb not her dream.

Thou stock-dove, whose echo resounds thro' the glen,
Ye wild whistling blackbirds in yon thorny den,
Thou green-crested lapwing, thy screaming forbear,
I charge you disturb not my slumbering fair.

How lofty, sweet Afton, thy neighbouring hills,
Far mark'd with the courses of clear winding rills;
There daily I wander as noon rises high,
My flocks and my Mary's sweet cot in my eye.

How pleasant thy banks and green valleys below,
Where wild in the woodlands the primroses blow;
There oft, as mild Ev'ning sweeps over the lea,
The sweet-scented birk shades my Mary and me.

Thy crystal stream, Afton, how lovely it glides,
And winds by the cot where my Mary resides,
How wanton thy waters her snowy feet lave,
As gathering sweet flowrets she stems thy clear wave.

Flow gently, sweet Afton, among thy green braes,
Flow gently, sweet river, the theme of my lays;
My Mary's asleep by thy murmuring stream,
Flow gently, sweet Afton, disturb not her dream.

11

THE SILVER TASSIE

A tassie is the Scots word for a cup or goblet. Parts of *The Silver Tassie* came from an old Jacobite ballad, originally published in the Scots Musical Museum. Bonnie Mary here is believed to be Mary Campbell, also referred to as Highland Mary.

Gae bring tae me a pint o' wine,
And fill it in a silver tassie,
That I may drink, before I go,
A service to my bonnie lassie.
The boat rocks at the pier o' Leith,
Fu' loud the winds blaws frae the ferry,
The ship rides by the Berwick Law,
And I maun leave my bonnie Mary.

The trumpets sound, the banner fly,
The glittering spears are ranked ready;
The shouts o' war are heard afar,
The battle closes deep and bloody !
It's no' the roar o' sea or shore
Wad mak' me langer wish to tarry,
Nor shouts o' war that's heard afar,
It's leaving thee, my bonnie Mary!

12

AULD LANG SYNE

By far the most well-known of the Bard's works, Burns acknowledged noting down some of the lyrics from an old man's song in 1788 before amending them himself to what we know now.

Auld Lang Syne is known the world over as a song of friendship and celebration. Throughout the western world it is traditionally sung on the stroke of twelve on New Year's Eve, or Hogmanay in Scotland.

Should auld acquaintance be forgot,
And never brought to mind?
Should auld acquaintance be forgot,
And auld lang syne!

Chorus…
For auld lang syne, my dear,
For auld lang syne.
We'll tak a cup o' kindness yet,
For auld lang syne.

And surely ye'll be your pint stowp!
And surely I'll be mine!
And we'll tak a cup o'kindness yet,
For auld lang syne.

Chorus...
We twa hae run about the braes,
And pou'd the gowans fine;
But we've wander'd mony a weary fit,
Sin' auld lang syne.

Chorus...
We twa hae paidl'd in the burn,
Frae morning sun till dine;
But seas between us braid hae roar'd
Sin' auld lang syne.

Chorus...
And there's a hand, my trusty fere!

And gie's a hand o' thine!
And we'll tak a right gude-willie waught,
For auld lang syne.

1

ADDRESS TO A HAGGIS

Written in 1786, Burns first recited this, apparently "off the cuff" when attending the dinner of a friend. Now it is a ritual part of any Burns Supper. The Haggis is paraded on a silver salver to the rousing music of the bagpipe before being handed over to an honored guest to 'address the haggis'. On the line "An' cut ye up wi' ready slight" the knife into the haggis.

Fair fa' your honest, sonsie face,
Great chieftain o' the puddin-race!
Aboon them a' ye tak your place,
Painch, tripe, or thairm:
Weel are ye wordy of a grace
As lang's my arm.

The groaning trencher there ye fill,
Your hudies like a distant hill,
Your pin wad help to mend a mill
In time o' need,
While thro' your pores the dews distil
Like amber bead.

His knife see rustic Labour dight,
An' cut ye up wi' ready slight,
Trenching your gushing entrails bright,
Like onie ditch;
And then, O what a glorious sight,
Warm-reeking, rich!

Then horn for horn, they stretch an' strive:
Deil tak the hindmost, on they drive,
Till a' their weel-swall'd kytes belyve
Are bent like drums;
Then auld Guidman, maist like to rive,
'Bethankit!' hums.

Is there that owre his French ragout,

Or olio that wad staw a sow,
Or fricassee wad mak her spew
Wi perfect scunner,
Looks down wi' sneering, scornfu' view
On sic a dinner?

Poor devil! see him owre his trash,
As fec'less as a wither'd rash,
His spindle shank a guid whip-lash,
His nieve a nit;
Tho' bluidy flood or field to dash,
O how unfit.

But mark the Rustic, haggis-fed,
The trembling earth resounds his tread,
Clap in his walie nieve a blade,
He'll make it whistle;
An' legs, an' arms, an' heads will sned
Like taps o' thrissle.

Ye pow'rs, wha mak mankind your care,
And dish them out their bill o' fare,
Auld Scotland wants nae skinking ware,
That jaups in luggies;
But if ye wish her gratfu' prayer,
Gie her a Haggis!

2

THE SELKIRK GRACE

Commonly said at a Burns Supper, the *Selkirk Grace* is first thought to have been recited by Burns when he had a meal with the Earl of Selkirk.

Some hae meat and canna eat,
And some would eat that want it;
But we hae meat, and we can eat,
Sae let the Lord be thankit.

3

TO A MOUSE

Written during his days as a farmer, Burns story of an evicted mouse is often seen as a parallel to his own situation at the time. As a tenant farmer, he too could be thrown out of his home at any time and left to face the elements. Over the years, the poem has held such sway as to be the source of the title for John Steinbeck's Of Mice and Men.

Wee, sleekit, cowrin, tim'rous beastie,
O, what a panic's in thy breastie!
Thou need na start awa sae hasty
Wi bickering brattle!
I wad be laith to rin an' chase thee,
Wi' murdering pattle.

I'm truly sorry man's dominion
Has broken Nature's social union,
An' justifies that ill opinion
Which makes thee startle
At me, thy poor, earth born companion
An' fellow mortal!

I doubt na, whyles, but thou may thieve;
What then? poor beastie, thou maun live!
A daimen icker in a thrave
'S a sma' request;
I'll get a blessin wi' the lave,
An' never miss't.

Thy wee-bit housie, too, in ruin!
It's silly wa's the win's are strewin!
An' naething, now, to big a new ane,
O' foggage green!
An' bleak December's win's ensuin,
Baith snell an' keen!

Thou saw the fields laid bare an' waste,
An' weary winter comin fast,

An' cozie here, beneath the blast,
Thou thought to dwell,
Till crash! the cruel coulter past
Out thro' thy cell.

That wee bit heap o' leaves an' stibble,
Has cost thee monie a weary nibble!
Now thou's turned out, for a' thy trouble,
But house or hald,
To thole the winter's sleety dribble,
An' cranreuch cauld.

But Mousie, thou art no thy lane,
In proving foresight may be vain:
The best laid schemes o' mice an' men
Gang aft agley,
An' lea'e us nought but grief an' pain,
For promis'd joy!

Still thou are blest, compared wi' me!
The present only toucheth thee:
But och! I backward cast my e'e,
On prospects drear!
An' forward, tho' I canna see,
I guess an' fear!

4

TO A MOUNTAIN DAISY

Originally titled 'The Gowan'. The poem tells of how the poet, while out with the plough, discovers that he has crushed a daisy's stem. It is also considered to be a commentary of Burns' then situation with Jean Armour who was forcibly being engaged to another, wealthier suitor.

Wee, modest crimson-tipped flow'r,
Thou's met me in an evil hour;
For I maun crush amang the stoure
Thy slender stem:
To spare thee now is past my pow'r,
Thou bonie gem.

Alas! it's no thy neibor sweet,
The bonie lark, companion meet,
Bending thee 'mang the dewy weet,
Wi' spreckl'd breast!
When upward-springing, blythe, to greet
The purpling east.

Cauld blew the bitter-biting north
Upon thy early, humble birth;
Yet cheerfully thou glinted forth
Amid the storm,
Scarce rear'd above the parent-earth
Thy tender form.

The flaunting flow'rs our gardens yield,
High shelt'ring woods and wa's maun shield;
But thou, beneath the random bield
O' clod or stane,
Adorns the histie stibble field,
Unseen, alane.

There, in thy scanty mantle clad,
Thy snawie bosom sun-ward spread,

Thou lifts thy unassuming head
In humble guise;
But now the share uptears thy bed,
And low thou lies!

Such is the fate of artless maid,
Sweet flow'ret of the rural shade!
By love's simplicity betray'd,
And guileless trust;
Till she, like thee, all soil'd, is laid
Low i' the dust.

Such is the fate of simple bard,
On life's rough ocean luckless starr'd!
Unskilful he to note the card
Of prudent lore,
Till billows rage, and gales blow hard,
And whelm him o'er!

Such fate to suffering worth is giv'n,
Who long with wants and woes has striv'n,
By human pride or cunning driv'n
To mis'ry's brink;
Till wrench'd of ev'ry stay but Heav'n,
He, ruin'd, sink!

Ev'n thou who mourn'st the Daisy's fate,
That fate is thine-no distant date;
Stern Ruin's plough-share drives elate,
Full on thy bloom,

Till crush'd beneath the furrow's weight,
Shall be thy doom!

5

HOLY WILLIE'S PRAYER

The poem is a satire based on a church elder named Fisher in the Parish church of Mauchline, in Ayrshire. Burns saw him as a hypocrite because while sinning in secret himself, he spied on other people and reported their misdeeds to the minister. The phrase "Holy Willie" has become part of the Scots language for someone who is both humourless and sanctimonious.

O Thou, that in the heavens does dwell,
As it pleases best Thysel',
Sends aen to Heaven an' ten to Hell,
For Thy glory,
And no for onie guid or ill
They've done afore Thee!

I bless and praise Thy matchless might,
When thousands Thou hast left in night,
That I am here afore Thy sight,
For gifts an' grace
A burning and a shining light
To a' this place.

What was I, or my generation,
That I should get sic exaltation?
I wha deserv'd most just damnation
For broken laws,
Six thousand years 'ere my creation,
Thro' Adam's cause.

When from my mither's womb I fell,
Thou might hae plung'd me deep in hell,
To gnash my gums, and weep and wail,
In burnin lakes,
Where damned devils roar and yell,
Chain'd to their stakes.

Yet I am here a chosen sample,
To show thy grace is great and ample;

I'm here a pillar o' Thy temple,
Strong as a rock,
A guide, a buckler, and example,
To a' Thy flock.

O Lord, Thou kens what zeal I bear,
When drinkers drink, an' swearers swear,
An' singing here, an' dancin there,
Wi' great and sma';
For I am keepit by Thy fear
Free frae them a'.

But yet, O Lord! confess I must,
At times I'm fash'd wi' fleshly lust:
An' sometimes, too, in worldly trust,
Vile self gets in;
But Thou remembers we are dust,
Defil'd wi' sin.

O Lord! yestreen, Thou kens, wi' Meg
Thy pardon I sincerely beg;
O may't ne'er be a livin' plague
To my dishonour,
An' I'll ne'er lift a lawless leg
Again upon her.

Besides, I farther maun avow,
Wi' Leezie's lass, three times I trow -
But Lord, that Friday I was fou,
When I cam near her;

Or else, Thou kens, Thy servant true
Wad never steer her.

Maybe Thou lets this fleshly thorn
Buffet Thy servant e'en and morn,
Lest he owre proud and high shou'd turn,
That he's sae gifted:
If sae, Thy han' maun e'en be borne,
Until Thou lift it.

Lord, bless Thy chosen in this place,
For here Thou has a chosen race!
But God confound there stuborn face,
An' blast their name,
Wha brings Thy elders to disgrace
An' open shame.

Lord, mind Gaw'n Hamilton's deserts;
He drinks, an' swears, an' plays at cartes,
Yet has sae mony takin arts,
Wi' great an' sma',
Frae God's ain priest the people's hearts
He steals awa'.

And when we chasten'd him therefore,
Thou kens how he bred sic a splore,
And set the world in a roar
O' laughing at us;
Curse Thou his basket and his store,
Kail an' potatoes.

Lord, hear my earnest cry and pray'r,
Against that Presbyt'ry o' Ayr;
Thy strong right hand, Lord mak it bare
Upo' their heads;
Lord visit them, an' dinna spare,
For their misdeeds.

O Lord my God! that glib-tongu'd Aitken,
My vera heart an' flesh are quakin,
To think how we stood sweatin, shakin,
An' pish'd wi' dread,
While he, wi' hingin lip an' snakin,
Held up his head.

Lord, in Thy day o' vengeance try him,
Lord, visit them wha did employ him,
And pass not in Thy mercy by them,
Nor hear their pray'r,
But for Thy people's sake destroy them,
An' dinna spare.

But, Lord, remember me an' mine
Wi' mercies temporal and divine,
That I for grace an' gear may shine,
Excell'd by nane,
And a' the glory shall be Thine,
Amen, Amen!

6

TO A LOUSE

To A Louse is another of Burn's poems written for the 'beasties' with another social twist to it. Whilst sitting behind a local beauty in church, he noticed the offending louse weaving its way through her hair. The woman believed the stares from the other parishioners were for her and her looks. In Burn's own words "O wad some Power the giftie gie us, to see oursels as ithers see us!"

Ha! Whare ye gaun, ye crowlin ferlie?
Your impudence protects you sairly,
I canna say but ye strut rarely
Owre gauze and lace,
Tho' faith! I fear ye dine but sparely
On sic a place.

Ye ugly, creepin, blastit wonner,
Detested, shunn'd by saunt an' sinner,
How daur ye set your fit upon her --
Sae fine a lady!
Gae somewhere else and seek your dinner
On some poor body.

Swith! in some beggar's hauffet squattle:
There you may creep, and sprawl, and spr
Wi' ither kindred, jumping cattle,
In shoals and nations;
Whare horn nor bane ne'er daur unsettle
Your thick plantations.

Now haud you there! ye're out o' sight,
Below the fatt'rils, snug an' tight;
Na, faith ye yet! ye'll no be right,
Till ye've got on it ---
The vera tapmost, tow'ring height
O' miss's bonnet.

My sooth! right bauld ye set your nose ou
As plump an' grey as onie grozet:

O for some rank, mercurial rozet,
Or fell, red smeddum,
I'd gie ye sic a hearty dose o't,
Wad dress your droddum!

I wad na been surpris'd to spy
You on an auld wife's flainen toy:
Or aiblins some bit duddie boy,
On's wyliecoat;
But Miss's fine Lunardi! fye!
How daur ye do't.

O Jenny, dinna toss your head,
An' set your beauties a' abread!
You little ken what cursed speed
The blastie's makin!
Thae winks an' finger-ends, I dread,
Are notice takin'!

O wad some Power the giftie gie us
To see oursels as ithers see us!
It wad frae monie a blunder free us,
An' foolish notion:
What airs in dress an' gait wad lea'e us,
An' ev'n devotion!

7

MARY MORISON

Another of The Bard's tributes to lost love; he is supposed to have proposed to Elison Begbie in the spring of 1784 only to have been refused. It is believed that as his love's name was not lyrically suitable, he replaced it in this piece with the name Mary Morison.

O Mary, at thy window be,
It is the wish'd, the trysted hour!
Those smiles and glances let me see,
That make the miser's treasure poor:
How blythely was I bide the stour,
A weary slave frae sun to sun,
Could I the rich reward secure,
The lovely Mary Morison.

Yestreen, when to the trembling string
The dance gaed thro' the lighted ha',
To thee my fancy took its wing,
I sat, but neither heard nor saw:
Tho' this was fair, and that was braw,
And yon the toast of a' the town,
I sigh'd, and said among them a',
"Ye are na Mary Morison."

Oh, Mary, canst thou wreck his peace,
Wha for thy sake wad gladly die?
Or canst thou break that heart of his,
Whase only faut is loving thee?
If love for love thou wilt na gie,
At least be pity to me shown;
A thought ungentle canna be
The thought o' Mary Morison.

8

TAM O SHANTER

Burns' magnificent epic is a Halloween tale of fantastic imagery where witches and wizards cavort through a stormy eve. First published in 1790, the tale is considered to be the Bard's finest poem and while usually recited in January to match with other celebrations, it really is a tale best suited for All Hallows Eve.

When chapman billies leave the street,
And drouthy neibors, neibors, meet;
As market days are wearing late,
And folk begin to tak the gate,
While we sit bousing at the nappy,
An' getting fou and unco happy,
We think na on the lang Scots miles,
The mosses, waters, slaps and stiles,
That lie between us and our hame,
Where sits our sulky, sullen dame,
Gathering her brows like gathering storm,
Nursing her wrath to keep it warm.

This truth fand honest Tam o' Shanter,
As he frae Ayr ae night did canter:
(Auld Ayr, wham ne'er a town surpasses,
For honest men and bonie lasses).

O Tam! had'st thou but been sae wise,
As taen thy ain wife Kate's advice!
She tauld thee weel thou was a skellum,
A blethering, blustering, drunken blellum;
That frae November till October,
Ae market-day thou was na sober;
That ilka melder wi' the Miller,
Thou sat as lang as thou had siller;
That ev'ry naig was ca'd a shoe on
The Smith and thee gat roarin' fou on;

That at the Lord's house, ev'n on Sunday,
Thou drank wi' Kirkton Jean till Monday,
She prophesied that late or soon,
Thou wad be found, deep drown'd in Doon,
Or catch'd wi' warlocks in the mirk,
By Alloway's auld, haunted kirk.

Ah, gentle dames! it gars me greet,
To think how mony counsels sweet,
How mony lengthen'd, sage advices,
The husband frae the wife despises!

But to our tale: Ae market night,
Tam had got planted unco right,
Fast by an ingle, bleezing finely,
Wi reaming swats, that drank divinely;
And at his elbow, Souter Johnie,
His ancient, trusty, drougthy crony:
Tam lo'ed him like a very brither;
They had been fou for weeks thegither.
The night drave on wi' sangs an' clatter;
And aye the ale was growing better:
The Landlady and Tam grew gracious,
Wi' favours secret, sweet, and precious:
The Souter tauld his queerest stories;
The Landlord's laugh was ready chorus:
The storm without might rair and rustle,
Tam did na mind the storm a whistle.

Care, mad to see a man sae happy,

E'en drown'd himsel amang the nappy.
As bees flee hame wi' lades o' treasure,
The minutes wing'd their way wi' pleasure:
Kings may be blest, but Tam was glorious,
O'er a' the ills o' life victorious!

But pleasures are like poppies spread,
You seize the flow'r, its bloom is shed;
Or like the snow falls in the river,
A moment white - then melts for ever;
Or like the Borealis race,
That flit ere you can point their place;
Or like the Rainbow's lovely form
Evanishing amid the storm. -
Nae man can tether Time nor Tide,
The hour approaches Tam maun ride;
That hour, o' night's black arch the key-stane,
That dreary hour he mounts his beast in;
And sic a night he taks the road in,
As ne'er poor sinner was abroad in.

The wind blew as 'twad blawn its last;
The rattling showers rose on the blast;
The speedy gleams the darkness swallow'd;
Loud, deep, and lang, the thunder bellow'd:
That night, a child might understand,
The deil had business on his hand.

Weel-mounted on his grey mare, Meg,
A better never lifted leg,

Tam skelpit on thro' dub and mire,
Despising wind, and rain, and fire;
Whiles holding fast his gude blue bonnet,
Whiles crooning o'er some auld Scots sonnet,
Whiles glow'rin round wi' prudent cares,
Lest bogles catch him unawares;
Kirk-Alloway was drawing nigh,
Where ghaists and houlets nightly cry.

By this time he was cross the ford,
Where in the snaw the chapman smoor'd;
And past the birks and meikle stane,
Where drunken Charlie brak's neck-bane;
And thro' the whins, and by the cairn,
Where hunters fand the murder'd bairn;
And near the thorn, aboon the well,
Where Mungo's mither hang'd hersel'.
Before him Doon pours all his floods,
The doubling storm roars thro' the woods,
The lightnings flash from pole to pole,
Near and more near the thunders roll,
When, glimmering thro' the groaning trees,
Kirk-Alloway seem'd in a bleeze,
Thro' ilka bore the beams were glancing,
And loud resounded mirth and dancing.

Inspiring bold John Barleycorn!
What dangers thou canst make us scorn!
Wi' tippenny, we fear nae evil;
Wi' usquabae, we'll face the devil!

The swats sae ream'd in Tammie's noddle,
Fair play, he car'd na deils a boddle,
But Maggie stood, right sair astonish'd,
Till, by the heel and hand admonish'd,
She ventur'd forward on the light;
And, wow! Tam saw an unco sight!

Warlocks and witches in a dance:
Nae cotillon, brent new frae France,
But hornpipes, jigs, strathspeys, and reels,
Put life and mettle in their heels.
A winnock-bunker in the east,
There sat auld Nick, in shape o' beast;
A towzie tyke, black, grim, and large,
To gie them music was his charge:
He screw'd the pipes and gart them skirl,
Till roof and rafters a' did dirl. -
Coffins stood round, like open presses,
That shaw'd the Dead in their last dresses;
And (by some devilish cantraip sleight)
Each in its cauld hand held a light.
By which heroic Tam was able
To note upon the haly table,
A murderer's banes, in gibbet-airns;
Twa span-lang, wee, unchristened bairns;
A thief, new-cutted frae a rape,
Wi' his last gasp his gab did gape;
Five tomahawks, wi' blude red-rusted:
Five scimitars, wi' murder crusted;
A garter which a babe had strangled:

A knife, a father's throat had mangled.
Whom his ain son of life bereft,
The grey-hairs yet stack to the heft;
Wi' mair of horrible and awfu',
Which even to name wad be unlawfu'.
Three lawyers tongues, turned inside oot,
Wi' lies, seamed like a beggars clout,
Three priests hearts, rotten, black as muck,
Lay stinkin, vile in every neuk.

As Tammie glowr'd, amaz'd, and curious,
The mirth and fun grew fast and furious;
The Piper loud and louder blew,
The dancers quick and quicker flew,
They reel'd, they set, they cross'd, they cleekit,
Till ilka carlin swat and reekit,
And coost her duddies to the wark,
And linkit at it in her sark!

Now Tam, O Tam! had they been queans,
A' plump and strapping in their teens!
Their sarks, instead o' creeshie flainen,
Been snaw-white seventeen hunder linen!-
Thir breeks o' mine, my only pair,
That ance were plush o' guid blue hair,
I wad hae gien them off my hurdies,
For ae blink o' the bonie burdies!
But wither'd beldams, auld and droll,
Rigwoodie hags wad spean a foal,
Louping an' flinging on a crummock.

I wonder did na turn thy stomach.

But Tam kent what was what fu' brawlie:
There was ae winsome wench and waulie
That night enlisted in the core,
Lang after ken'd on Carrick shore;
(For mony a beast to dead she shot,
And perish'd mony a bonie boat,
And shook baith meikle corn and bear,
And kept the country-side in fear);
Her cutty sark, o' Paisley harn,
That while a lassie she had worn,
In longitude tho' sorely scanty,
It was her best, and she was vauntie.
Ah! little ken'd thy reverend grannie,
That sark she coft for her wee Nannie,
Wi twa pund Scots ('twas a' her riches),
Wad ever grac'd a dance of witches!

But here my Muse her wing maun cour,
Sic flights are far beyond her power;
To sing how Nannie lap and flang,
(A souple jade she was and strang),
And how Tam stood, like ane bewithc'd,
And thought his very een enrich'd:
Even Satan glowr'd, and fidg'd fu' fain,
And hotch'd and blew wi' might and main:
Till first ae caper, syne anither,
Tam tint his reason a thegither,
And roars out, "Weel done, Cutty-sark!"

And in an instant all was dark:
And scarcely had he Maggie rallied.
When out the hellish legion sallied.

As bees bizz out wi' angry fyke,
When plundering herds assail their byke;
As open pussie's mortal foes,
When, pop! she starts before their nose;
As eager runs the market-crowd,
When "Catch the thief!" resounds aloud;
So Maggie runs, the witches follow,
Wi' mony an eldritch skreich and hollow.

Ah, Tam! Ah, Tam! thou'll get thy fairin!
In hell, they'll roast thee like a herrin!
In vain thy Kate awaits thy comin!
Kate soon will be a woefu' woman!
Now, do thy speedy-utmost, Meg,
And win the key-stone o' the brig;
There, at them thou thy tail may toss,
A running stream they dare na cross.

But ere the keystane she could make,
The fient a tail she had to shake!
For Nannie, far before the rest,
Hard upon noble Maggie prest,
And flew at Tam wi' furious ettle;
But little wist she Maggie's mettle!
Ae spring brought off her master hale,
But left behind her ain grey tail:

The carlin claught her by the rump,
And left poor Maggie scarce a stump.

Now, wha this tale o' truth shall read,
Ilk man and mother's son, take heed:
Whene'er to Drink you are inclin'd,
Or Cutty-sarks rin in your mind,
Think ye may buy the joys o'er dear;
Remember Tam o' Shanter's mare.

ABOUT THE EDITOR

Elizabeth Hepburn is a director of Scottish Traditional Music label, *Footstompin' Records.* For the past fifteen years, she has championed Scottish culture through forums, award-winning music and traditional literature.

Made in United States
Cleveland, OH
26 September 2025